HELEN-PLUM MEMORIAL LIBRARY
3 1502 00684 9176

D1790262

Y BIOG BON

Kallen, Stuart A., 1955-
Bono

Please check all items for damages
before leaving the Library.
Thereafter you will be held
responsible for all injuries
to items beyond reasonable wear.

Helen M. Plum Memorial Library

Lombard, Illinois

A daily fine will be charged for
overdue materials.

MAY 2009

MODERN ROLE MODELS

Bono

Stuart A. Kallen

Mason Crest Publishers

Produced by OTTN Publishing in association with
21st Century Publishing and Communications, Inc.

Copyright © 2009 by Mason Crest Publishers. All rights reserved. No part of this publication may be reproduced or transmitted in any form or by any means, electronic or mechanical, including photocopying, recording, taping, or any information storage and retrieval system, without permission from the publisher.

MASON CREST PUBLISHERS INC.
370 Reed Road
Broomall, Pennsylvania 19008
(866) MCP-BOOK (toll free)
www.masoncrest.com

Printed in the United States of America.

First Printing

9 8 7 6 5 4 3 2 1

Library of Congress Cataloging-in-Publication Data

Kallen, Stuart A., 1955–
  Bono / Stuart A. Kallen.
    p. cm. — (Modern role models)
ISBN-13: 978-1-4222-0499-3 (hardcover) — ISBN-13: 978-1-4222-0786-4 (pbk.)
 1. Bono, 1960– —Juvenile literature. 2. Rock musicians—Biography—Juvenile literature. I. Title.
ML3930.B592K35 2008
782.42166092—dc22   2008020419

Publisher's note:
All quotations in this book come from original sources, and contain the spelling and grammatical inconsistencies of the original text.

CROSS-CURRENTS

In the ebb and flow of the currents of life we are each influenced by many people, places, and events that we directly experience or have learned about. Throughout the chapters of this book you will come across **CROSS-CURRENTS** *reference boxes. These boxes direct you to a* **CROSS-CURRENTS** *section in the back of the book that contains fascinating and informative sidebars and related pictures. Go on.* ▶▶

Contents

1 The Liberty Medal — 5

2 Becoming Bono — 11

3 A Band with a Conscience — 17

4 Pop and Politics — 27

5 The Most Powerful Man in Music — 37

Cross-Currents — 48

Chronology — 55

Accomplishments & Awards — 56

Further Reading & Internet Resources — 59

Glossary — 60

Notes — 61

Index — 63

Picture Credits — 64

About the Author — 64

On September 27, 2007, the National Constitution Center's 2007 Liberty Medal was awarded jointly to Bono, U2 lead singer and activist, and DATA (Debt, AIDS, Trade, Africa), the advocacy organization he cofounded to combat poverty and disease in Africa. The ceremony took place at the National Constitution Center, located in Philadelphia, Pennsylvania.

1

The Liberty Medal

THE NATIONAL CONSTITUTIONAL CENTER USUALLY awards its esteemed Liberty Medal to presidents, kings, and Supreme Court justices. But in September 2007 it gave the award to an Irish rock star. Bono was the first entertainer to receive the medal. He was chosen because he also has become a respected leader in the fight to end African poverty and disease.

Bono is a man who maintains two demanding careers. He is the lead singer and **front man** in the band U2. And he is a tireless advocate for the poor and powerless. When he accepted the Liberty Award he spoke movingly about a troubled world:

> "[When] you are trapped by poverty, you are not free. When trade laws prevent you from selling the food you grew, you are not free. When you are dying of a mosquito bite, for lack of a bed net, you are not

> free. When you are hungry in a world of plenty, you are not free. When you are a monk in Burma this very week, barred from entering a temple because of your gospel of peace . . . well, then *none of us* are truly free."

Bono, whose band made over $225 million in 2005, donated the $100,000 prize to DATA, a charitable group he had helped found in 2002 and that shared the award.

"Bono Understands His Issues"

DATA stands for Debt, AIDS, Trade, Africa. The organization raises money to treat AIDS patients. It convinces banks to forgive huge loans made to African nations. And it works to break down trade barriers so Africans can sell their products on the world market. All this is meant to help lift 1 billion Africans out of extreme poverty, strengthen democracy, and eliminate brutal wars.

Such complicated bureaucratic issues are usually handled by ambassadors, bankers, lawyers, and economists. But Bono uses his popularity to focus the world's attention on these problems. And he uses more than celebrity and personal charm to advance DATA's goals. As conservative Pennsylvania senator Rick Santorum told *Time* magazine:

> "If you really want to be effective, you have to bring something to the table beyond just **charisma**. The important thing is, Bono understands his issues better than 99% of members of Congress."

Knowing the issues helps Bono achieve results. In 2005 he attended the G8 summit, a gathering of the world's most powerful leaders from the eight richest nations in North America, Europe, and Asia. After he met with five heads of state, the G8 approved a record $25 billion in aid to Africa. The organization

> **CROSS-CURRENTS**
> AIDS is taking a terrible toll on the continent of Africa today. For some facts, see "AIDS in Africa." Go to page 48.

> **CROSS-CURRENTS**
> To find out more about the Group of Eight, which includes the world's wealthiest nations, check out "Bono and the G8." Go to page 49.

The Liberty Medal

Overseas Development Minister of State for Ireland Tom Kitt (left) and Bono walk by Dublin Castle, the site of a European Union conference on development aid. Kitt invited Bono to attend the conference, held in June 2004, because the Irish rock star had been a longtime advocate of providing aid to developing countries in Africa.

also promised to provide inexpensive anti-AIDS drugs to 10 million afflicted Africans.

"I Try to Live It"

When asked about the driving force behind his charity work, Bono credits his Christian **commitment** to the poor. He adheres to the principles outlined in the Bible and quoted scripture to President George W. Bush when the two met in 2002. Impressed by Bono's depth of commitment, Bush moved to fund programs that provide millions of American dollars for African AIDS relief. Bono explained his Christian faith to *Time*:

> "I try to live it rather than talk about it because there are enough secondhand-car salesmen for

> God. But I cannot escape my conviction that God is interested in the progress of mankind, individually and collectively."

Beyond his religious convictions, Bono uses his rock-and-roll stardom to get things done. For example, before the 2005 G8 summit, the singer organized a series of free concerts in London, Paris, Moscow, Philadelphia, Rome, Ontario, and elsewhere. Called Live 8, the concerts were broadcast on 182 television networks and were seen by an estimated 3 billion people, or half the world's

At the final concert of the Live 8 performances, held on July 6, 2005, in Edinburgh, Scotland, Bono holds the petition of more than 30 million names calling on world leaders to increase aid and cancel debt for the poorest countries in Africa. The Live 8 List was presented to UK prime minister Tony Blair, who chaired the G8 meeting.

population. Bono was able to persuade the biggest stars in music to take part, including Coldplay, Madonna, Paul McCartney, Mariah Carey, Snoop Dogg, Linkin Park, Ludacris, Maroon 5, and Snow Patrol. Bono was even able to convince the long-feuding members of Pink Floyd to reunite for the first time in 24 years. Bono comments on the success of the concert on the Live 8 Web site:

> **Live 8 was, and remains a brilliant moment but what is more important is the brilliant movement of which it was a part. This gives the poorest of the poor real political muscle for the first time. . . . It is this movement, not rock stars, that will make it [impossible] in the future to break promises to the most vulnerable people on this planet.**

PERSON OF THE YEAR

Bono's whirlwind of good works attracted the attention of *Time*, which named him Person of the Year in 2005. Bono shared the honor with Microsoft billionaire Bill Gates and his wife, Melinda. The Gateses had started the world's most well-funded charity, the Bill and Melinda Gates **Foundation**, with a $29 billion endowment. Some of the money from the foundation helped Bono launch DATA. Together, Bono and the Gateses were responsible for a host of efficient, well-run medical programs meant to help Africa's poorest citizens. Their efforts reduced deaths from tuberculosis, AIDS, malaria, and complications from pregnancy.

Thousands of people owe their lives to Bono and the Gateses, who joined forces for purely unselfish reasons. And Bono has achieved amazing results by asking everyone from average citizens to world leaders to join his cause to end poverty. As he told a group of bankers in 2007, "You, too, can make a difference." And the lead singer of U2 has made a difference, too.

Bono, whose real name is Paul David Hewson, was born and raised in Dublin, Ireland. The son of a postal worker and homemaker, he was a rebellious youth who often clashed with his father, especially after the early death of his mother. Music would provide a welcome outlet for the troubled teen.

2

Becoming Bono

BONO HAS PLAYED ON STAGES ACROSS THE GLOBE. He has shaken hands with kings, popes, presidents, and prime ministers. And he socializes with some of the world's richest people. As a young man, however, Bono grew up in a rough neighborhood in Dublin, Ireland, where gangs ran loose through dirty streets and feelings of hopelessness filled the air.

⇛ Growing Up in Ireland ⇚

Bono was born in Dublin's Rotunda Hospital on May 10, 1960. His parents, Iris and Bobby Hewson, named their second son Paul David Hewson. Although their neighborhood was considered rough, the Hewsons lived in a newly built three-bedroom house. Iris was Protestant, and Bobby was Catholic.

Paul and his older brother, Norman, attended the all-male Protestant Asnevin National School. Norman was a model student who got good grades. Paul, however, was another story. Even at a young age he was unruly, stubborn, and ready to fight for what he believed.

Paul was naturally drawn to music, particularly the guitar-heavy music of Jimi Hendrix and the Who. The rebellious rock fueled Paul's hostility toward society. During the 1971 school year, he stopped attending classes and spent his days wandering the streets of Dublin. He often got into trouble for committing petty crimes.

Paul's frustrated parents believed their son needed a fresh start at a new school. They sent Paul to Mount Temple High School, which was much more liberal than Asnevin. There was no dress code, so Paul no longer had to wear his hated school uniform. The school accepted both boys and girls and took Catholic and Protestant students. This was seen as very forward thinking. At the time, Dublin was bitterly divided along religious lines. A period of violence, called the Troubles, had begun between Catholics and Protestants in Northern Ireland in 1968. This ongoing conflict drove a wedge between Irish people of different religious backgrounds, even in the Republic of Ireland where the Hewsons lived.

> **CROSS-CURRENTS**
> Conflicts between Protestants and Catholics in Ireland have occurred for centuries. To learn more, read "Religious Tensions in Ireland." Go to page 50.

A Tragic Loss

In the less-restrictive atmosphere at Mount Temple, Paul transformed into a popular, talkative, and intelligent student. He was a good painter, excelled in history, and his outgoing personality made him a natural actor in school plays.

Paul's life took a heartbreaking turn on September 10, 1974, when his mother died unexpectedly of a brain aneurysm. Paul was devastated by his mother's death, and once again he began to rebel. He dyed his hair red and took to wearing outrageous outfits. And while he had always clashed with his father and brother, their arguments grew increasingly fierce.

> **CROSS-CURRENTS**
> To read Bono's account of living at home after his mother's death, check out "About as Low as You Can Get." Go to page 51.

Paul found a new channel for his rebellious ways in 1976. Around that time a new form of music, known as **punk** rock, was becoming popular. The angry, fast-paced rock and roll immediately appealed to Paul. He began learning the songs and teaching himself to sing and play guitar.

⇶ Paul Becomes Bono ⇇

Because some famous punk rockers adopted made-up names, Paul also decided to take a new name. A friend suggested that because Paul had a loud singing voice, he should call himself Bono Vox. (The words roughly translate from Latin to mean "good voice.") Paul felt

In the fall of 1976, four teenagers with limited musical experience founded a band that would eventually become known as U2. They were, from left to right, Adam Clayton (bass guitar), Paul "Bono" Hewson (vocals and guitar), Larry Mullen, Jr. (drums, percussion, and vocals), and David "The Edge" Evans (guitar, keyboards, and vocals).

BONO

During the late 1970s, Bono's band appeared under the name of Hype or Feedback at venues in and around Dublin. Because of its charismatic, high-energy performances, the group quickly attracted numerous fans. By 1978 it had adopted the name U2 and moved from performing covers to mostly playing music written by Bono and other band members.

the name was too long and dropped the "Vox." He was thereafter known simply as Bono (pronounced Bon-oh, not Bone-oh).

Despite the meaning of his new name, Bono did not have a very good voice. He did, however, possess a great amount of charm. On September 25, 1976, he answered an ad seeking a vocalist posted by 15-year-old drummer Larry Mullen Jr. on a school bulletin board. Bono showed up for a jam in Larry's kitchen, which was attended by bassist Adam Clayton and guitarist Dave Evans, who earned the nickname "the Edge" for his angular facial features. Bono was not the best singer, and his guitar playing was terrible. But his loud voice, stage presence, and ability to create lyrics won him a spot in the band.

➤ THE FIRST BIG BREAK ➤

At first the band tried playing covers—that is, songs previously recorded by other bands. Since they did not have the skills to imitate pop stars, they decided to make up their own music using Bono's poetry for lyrics. Inspired by the power chords of the Who and the edgy lyrics of folk rocker Neil Young, the band began to forge its own sound. There was one problem, however. The band members were inexperienced amateurs who could barely play.

Within a year, however, the band had improved enough to develop a small but dedicated local following. On St. Patrick's Day 1978 the band had its first big break. It won a talent contest in the city of Limerick. The prize was about $1,500 and studio recording time. There were some issues, however, with the band's name. It had played for a time as Hype, then as Feedback (for the screeching noises emitted by Edge's abused guitar amp). Neither name seemed to suit the band. Finally, Adam's friend Steve Averill, who was a punk rocker, suggested U2, and the name stuck.

In April 1978 U2 used the studio time it won to record a **demo** tape to demonstrate its talents to record companies. The band members were unhappy with the result, and it went unused. It would not be until August 1979 that they would release their first record, *U2:3*. The short album contained three of the band's best original tunes. The band's eager fans in Dublin quickly purchased every available copy. This attracted the attention of **record producers** in London. Although the band members had only recently graduated from Mount Temple High, they were ready for stardom.

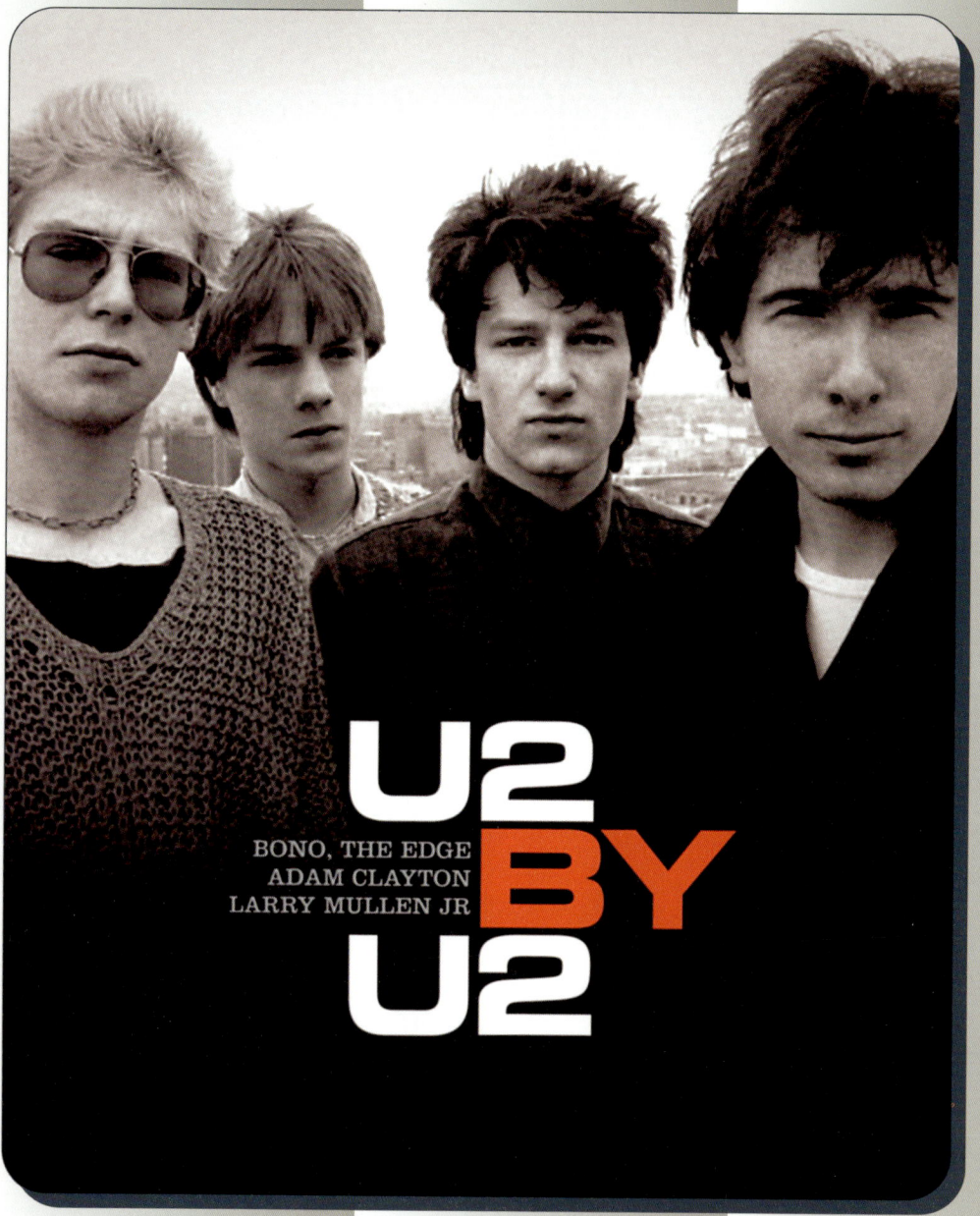

An early portrait of the four members of U2 appears on the cover of the band's history, *U2 by U2*, published in 2006. The group became famous during the 1980s for its innovative style and passionate idealism. That belief in the power of rock and roll to change the world would carry it to success in the years to come.

3

A Band with a Conscience

BONO TURNED TWENTY IN MAY 1980, AND HE received a perfect birthday present. U2's first single, "11 O'Clock Tick Tock" had just been released. Critics loved Bono's soaring vocals, the Edge's echoing guitar, and Mullen and Clayton's driving rhythm section. There was a unique sound on the airwaves, and it was U2.

The new song was released by Island Records, which had signed a recording contract earlier that year with the band. U2 was a perfect fit for Island. It was a respected independent record company, internationally famous as the musical home of reggae pioneer Bob Marley. Island nurtured artists to develop their own style, and U2 was striving for a sound like no other.

➤ Sad Words and Rollicking Music ➤

Island released U2's first album, *Boy*, in September 1980. Bono wrote all the lyrics on the album and most reflected a tragic sense of loss. For example, "I Will Follow" described the heartbreak he felt when his mother died. While the words may be **somber**, the rollicking music on the record is loud and energetic. The thundering mix of punk rock and radio-friendly pop music obscures the sadness found in Bono's lyrics.

Boy was a modest success, reaching number 52 on the British record charts. When it was released in the United States in early 1981, it only climbed to number 63. But U2 was slowly building an American audience. The band spent most of 1981 touring America, playing small clubs and auditoriums. The extensive travel was hard on the band. But the gigs exposed U2 to an eager new audience. "I Will Follow" was soon a hit on college radio stations throughout America.

"Gloria" and Ali

While on tour in the United States, Bono spent much of his time between shows on a run-down tour bus reading his Bible. Under pressure to write lyrics for U2's second album, he used the Bible as a guide and wrote songs with religious themes. The album *October* was released in October 1981, and it proved to be a breakthrough record for the band in the United Kingdom. Propelled by standout tracks such as "October" and "Gloria," the group's second album quickly sold more than 60,000 copies.

Despite the band's growing popularity, some critics panned *October*. The band's musical performance on the album was considered weak. The religious lyrics were called overbearing. However, the video for "Gloria" received a great deal of airplay on MTV. The music television station had only recently begun broadcasting. As it grew in popularity, so did interest in the brash new band from Ireland.

Bono took time away from his rock-and-roll career in August 1982 to marry his high school sweetheart, Ali Stewart. The couple had been dating since November 1975. Stewart was there at the formation of U2. And she cared for Bono during his darkest moments after his mother died. Ali and Bono's marriage would prove to be long lasting. They have four children and celebrated their 25th anniversary in 2007.

"Warrior-Rock Spirit"

In February 1983 U2 released its third album, *War*. For this album, Bono left behind the religious and personal lyrics and became openly political. The song "Sunday Bloody Sunday" kicks off the album with a militaristic drumbeat. Based on words and a guitar riff by the Edge, the song is about a violent episode in Northern Ireland. In January

A Band with a Conscience

Tours promoting U2's first album, *Boy*, took the band to cities in the United Kingdom, the United States, Sweden, France, Switzerland, and the Netherlands in late 1980 and the first half of 1981. While on the road, Bono wrote many of the songs that would be featured on the group's second album, *October*.

1972 the British army opened fire on a crowd of thousands of peaceful Catholic protesters, killing 13 and wounding 17. Many thought the song supported the violent Catholic rebels who were fighting the British. But Bono repeatedly has made it clear that "Sunday Bloody Sunday" is a call for peace.

BONO

U2 first played "Sunday Bloody Sunday" in 1982 in Belfast, Ireland, where the shooting took place. In 1983 the band released a video of U2 performing "Sunday Bloody Sunday" at the beautiful Red Rocks Amphitheatre in Colorado's Rocky Mountains. The video went into heavy rotation on MTV and further boosted U2's popularity. In 2004 *Rolling Stone* magazine said that the video performance was one of 50 moments that changed rock history:

U2's third album, *War*, released in 1983, reflects the band's decision to create music that made strong political statements. The album, which entered the charts in the United Kingdom at number one, includes the songs "Sunday Bloody Sunday," and "40," which confront "the Troubles"—the violence occurring between Protestants and Catholics in Ireland.

A Band with a Conscience

> **"The sight of Bono singing the anti-violence anthem 'Sunday Bloody Sunday' while waving a white flag through crimson mist (created by a combination of wet weather, hot lights and the illumination of those crags) became the defining image of U2's warrior-rock spirit and—shown in heavy rotation on MTV—broke the band nationwide."**

Propelled by the video, *War* sold more than 500,000 copies, giving U2 its first **gold record**. The live performance of the song was later released with seven other songs from the *War* tour on the eight-song album *Under a Blood Red Sky*. This album, and a concert video of the same name, captured the excitement of U2 live. The CD sold more than a million copies in the United States, giving U2 its first **platinum** album. The record sold 3 million copies in England and remains the best-selling concert album in British history. It also helped make Bono and his bandmates millionaires.

> **CROSS-CURRENTS**
>
> One of U2's most memorable concerts occurred in 1983. For details about this show, read "The All-Time Best Performance." Go to page 52. ▶▶

"We Broke Up the Band"

The success of *Under a Blood Red Sky* established U2 as one of the premier rock-and-roll bands of the era. *Rolling Stone* editors voted the band the Top Rock Act of 1983. However, Bono feared U2 was becoming known as a loud, angry, arena-rock band. For that reason, he did not want to repeat the same musical formula that made *War* a success.

To get a different sound, U2 sought new record producers. These people would organize the recording sessions and coach and guide band members with new ideas. For this important task, the band chose British producer Brian Eno, who was famous for his work as a **synthesizer** and keyboard player for the 1970s art-rock band Roxy Music. Eno had also worked with superstar David Bowie and with David Byrne, the leader of famed punk-rock band Talking Heads. The band also signed Canadian producer, writer, and guitarist Daniel Lanois to assist Eno. Together, these men would reshape U2's sound on 1984's *The Unforgettable Fire*.

Eno encouraged Bono to write lyrics that were less **moralistic** and more poetic. He also changed the band's hard-charging sound. On the title track, "The Unforgettable Fire," Eno recorded layers of spacey digital keyboards to create a calm, flowing sound. Commenting on the complete change in U2's approach, Bono tells *Rolling Stone*:

> **"We broke up the band after *War*. We literally broke up the band and formed another band with the same name and the same members."**

One song, however, "Pride (in the Name of Love)" reflected U2 at its *War*-time energetic best. Bono wrote the song to honor assassinated civil rights leader Martin Luther King Jr., and "Pride" became the band's biggest hit to date. When *The Unforgettable Fire* was released, it immediately entered the British charts at number one and had similar success in the United States, eventually selling 3 million copies and earning triple-platinum status.

U2 at Live Aid

The release of the album was followed by *The Unforgettable Fire* tour. This was a series of 113 concerts that took place between August 1984 and July 1985. Despite wanting to be seen as something other than a loud arena band, U2 was now so popular that it had to continue playing large venues, which often sold out in hours.

The last show of the tour was the Live Aid concert at London's Wembley Stadium on July 13, 1985. This was the biggest show of the tour and the first time the band played to help the poor in Africa. Live Aid was organized by Irish singer Bob Geldof to raise millions for Ethiopian famine relief. In the days before the concert, U2 issued the following statement explaining its participation in the event:

> **"U2 are involved in Live Aid because it's more than money, it's music—but it is also a demonstration to the politicians and policy-makers that men, women and children will not walk by men, women and children as they lie, bellies swollen, starving to death for the sake of a cup of grain and some water."**

Live Aid took place in stadiums in London, Philadelphia, Australia, and Japan and featured superstars such as Madonna, Bowie, Sting, Queen, and the Who. Despite the big-name lineup,

A Band with a Conscience

Constant touring and a string of hits helped U2 develop a large, devoted following in the United Kingdom and the United States during the early 1980s. By January 1985, when the magazine *Musician* featured the rock band on its cover, U2 was considered one of the world's top rock bands.

BONO

Bono soars during a benefit concert for Live Aid, held July 13, 1985, at Wembley Stadium, London. U2's dominant performance at the event is considered a defining moment in ensuring the rock band's worldwide fame. The concerts, held in London and in Philadelphia, raised millions of dollars for famine relief in Africa.

critics agree U2 stole the show. During a 13-minute version of "Bad," Bono clamored down from the high stage. He pushed his way past security, grabbed a girl from the audience, and pulled her onstage to dance. This move somehow made a magical connection with tens of millions of people watching the show at home on television. It is considered a pivotal moment in the band's career.

"Rock's Hottest Ticket"

Live Aid was the first in a series of benefit concerts played by U2. In 1986 U2 was the headliner for the "Conspiracy of Hope" tour held by the human rights organization Amnesty International. The six-show tour played to sold-out arenas across the United States and helped Amnesty International triple its membership.

Bono's interest in world affairs went beyond charity concerts. In 1986 he and Ali traveled to Nicaragua to provide money for a program that helped starving peasants caught in a civil war there. During their travels, they dodged bullets and bombs and witnessed war crimes.

Bono's grim experiences in Central America inspired his lyrics on U2's next album, *The Joshua Tree*. In "Bullet the Blue Sky," Bono sings about airplanes strafing peasant villages while the Edge imitates bombs whistling with his shrieking guitar. Two other songs on *The Joshua Tree*, "With or Without You" and "I Still Haven't Found What I'm Looking For," gave U2 its first number-one singles in the United States. The group made the cover of *Time* magazine with a headline that labeled it "Rock's Hottest Ticket." *The Joshua Tree* debuted at number one in Britain and quickly hit number one in the United States.

> **CROSS-CURRENTS**
> Over the years Bono has visited several war zones. To learn more about one trip, see "Civil War in Nicaragua." Go to page 52.

As the 1980s drew to a close, there was little doubt that Bono was one of the biggest rock stars in history. He was rich, he was famous, and nearly everyone wanted to hear him sing. But Bono was something more. Although he loved the perks of fame, he held on to his morals and beliefs. During a decade known for its greed and excess, Bono's marriage remained strong. And his commitment to the world's poorest people was unshakable.

The 1990s saw U2 reinvent itself as a pop rock band heavily influenced by dance, techno, and electronic music—sounds reflected in albums such as *Achtung Baby* and *Zooropa*. U2 produced more of the same in the 1997 album *Pop*. The band promoted its music with elaborately-staged multimedia tours held around the world.

Pop and Politics

IN 1992 U2 RELEASED *ACHTUNG BABY* AND HIT the road with its Zoo TV tour. The tour featured digital sounds, shrieking industrial guitars, and high-tech, electronic gadgetry. The stage was dominated by 36 video monitors filled with dozens of images, including those from the singer's handheld "Bono Cam." No one had ever seen anything like it.

The Zoo TV tour required 52 semitrucks to move the equipment from city to city and 200 laborers to construct the stage. Although the expenses for such a setup were high, U2 could do whatever it wanted. The band had signed a multimillion-dollar deal with Island Records and had complete freedom over its record, tour, and video production. Rock's Hottest Ticket of the 1980s was holding on to that title well into the 1990s as the group piled up awards from the National Academy of Recording Arts and Sciences, MTV, and *Rolling Stone*.

BONO

✦ "ON TO THE NEXT CENTURY" ✦

U2 continued to break new musical ground throughout the decade. *Zooropa*, produced by Eno in 1993, took the experimental sound of *Achtung Baby* to new levels. The album featured ambient electronic sounds and European **techno**-dance music. Despite no strong single, *Zooropa* eventually sold 8 million copies.

It would be four years before U2 released *Pop*, its ninth studio album. In the years between *Zooropa* and *Pop*, Bono did not sit idle. In fact, his dedication to social justice issues continued to grow. In 1995 he worked with opera singer Luciano Pavarotti to raise money for

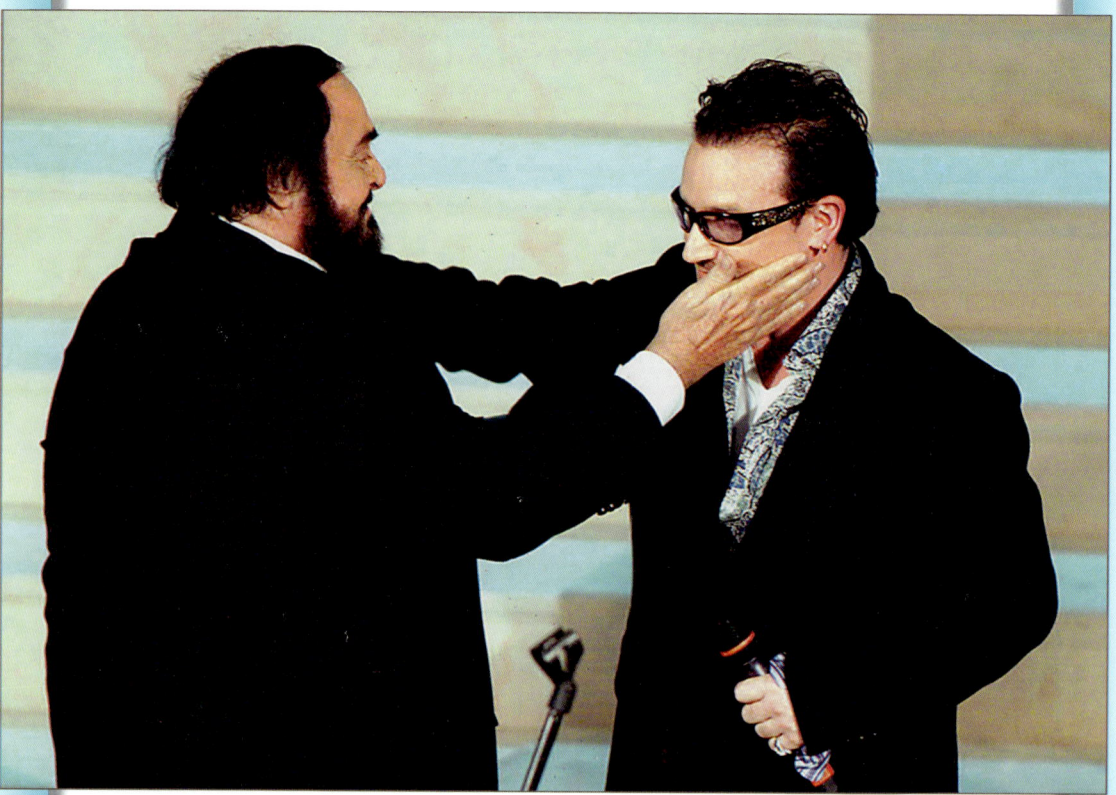

Bono worked with Italian opera star Luciano Pavarotti (left) in other charitable efforts besides War Child. This photograph was taken in February 2000, at the San Remo Festival, which was cohosted by Pavarotti. When the U2 rock star appeared at the festival's grand finale, he thanked Italian leaders for supporting the campaign for Third World debt forgiveness.

Pop and Politics

War Child. This organization was founded to protect children caught in wars around the world. The unlikely collaboration between the opera star and the rock singer resulted in the album *Pavarotti and Friends: Together for the Children of Bosnia*. Eno was the guiding force behind the album and later persuaded Bono and the Edge to play a concert with Pavarotti in Italy. The video of the event raised $6 million, and the money was used to provide musical instruments and build a musical therapy center for children of the war in Bosnia.

In 1998 Bono campaigned for peace closer to home when U2 played a concert in Belfast for the "Yes" campaign. The show was held to urge warring factions in Northern Ireland to vote yes on the Good Friday Peace Accord, meant to end the civil war. Commenting on the issue, Bono told reporters at the time:

> **To vote no is to play into the hands of the extremists who've had their day. Their day is over as far as we're concerned. We're on to the next century here.**

"Obscene and Not Acceptable"

In 1999, with the new century only one year away, Bono's work for Africa began to overshadow his role in U2. The singer and his wife had been involved in alleviating African poverty since he first traveled to Ethiopia in 1985. On subsequent trips, the problems became much more personal. During their African travels, Bono and Ali slept in tents and worked in orphanages and refugee camps, where they met homeless and starving men, women, and children.

Bono's work in Africa led him to develop a lifelong commitment to helping end poverty and starvation. In *U2 by U2*, Bono explained the origins of the debt crisis and how it inspired him to get involved with relief:

> **Ali and I had been to Africa . . . and had our hearts broken by the everyday tragedy that was life on that shining continent, the waste of lives and opportunity. We had a sense . . . that a lot of Africa's problems were not just natural calamity or war and warlords but some of the poverty problems were structural [resulting from the way the political**

> system was set up]. Corruption was a big problem, obviously, corrupt leaders and tinpot dictators. . . . But there was also corruption on the part of the developed world. The West, for its own strategic reasons, had loaned huge sums of money to Africa . . . often to very mad and very bad men. . . . These people . . . had squandered the countries' resources on personal enrichment and now the western world was holding ransom to the children of these choices made years and years before.
>
> This was obscene and not acceptable. . . . The injustice of it really struck a chord with me. [Debt relief] wasn't a charity-based idea, it was a justice-based idea. It made me think there was something solid we could do to change the lives of the people we'd met."

Bono came to understand that mass starvation was a result of politics, not food shortages. The problem could be traced back to the 1970s and 1980s, when irresponsible African leaders borrowed large sums of money from Western banks. Long after the money was squandered or stolen by dictators, the countries were left with astounding loan and interest payments that totaled more than $100 million a day. With most of the money going to banks, there was nothing left to feed, clothe, and educate the poorest people on Earth. The problems were compounded by the alarming spread of HIV/AIDS due to a lack of medicine.

Drop the Debt

The faith-based international organization Jubilee 2000 was founded in the late 1990s to erase African debt by the year 2000. Bono lent his voice to the group's Drop the Debt campaign in 1999. To learn more about the debt situation, he studied with Harvard professor Jeffrey Sachs.

Bono drew attention to the Jubilee 2000 campaign when he hosted a worldwide online interview from Dublin. The event was viewed by more than 2 million people. With Bono's help, Jubilee soon collected more than 21 million signatures on a petition calling on world leaders to cancel African debt. Bono personally presented

Pop and Politics

Bono became involved with African debt relief after he and his wife, Ali Hewson, traveled to Africa in 1985 and witnessed severe poverty firsthand. This photograph of Bono and Ali was taken in May 2006, during a visit to a rural clinic in Lesotho. The two were on a six-nation journey through Africa to highlight progress being made in treating people with HIV/AIDS.

the petition to Kofi Annan, the secretary-general of the United Nations. He also spoke before the U.S. Congress and convinced Pope John Paul II to get involved with debt relief. In an interview with CNN.com, Bono commented on his unusual role in Jubilee 2000:

> "I was part of the Jubilee 2000 Drop the Debt campaign, and the issue of poverty in the poorest countries in the world is completely bound up in health and education. In fact, there's still more of the poorest countries spending more on their

> debts, their old debts, than on health and education. . . . I really would rather not be here in the sense that I know how absurd it is having to listen to a rock star talk about [African debt relief]. But the truth of it is that politics and pop are very similar . . . so I guess I'm the person to try and, you know, sort of try to bring in the wider public."

Bono's ability to merge his pop star persona and politics paid off. As a result of his work with American politicians, the United States agreed to cancel nearly half a billion dollars in African debt.

"This Is Church"

After doing his work for Jubilee 2000, Bono felt it was time to leave the work of saving the planet to those with more experience. Besides, other members of U2 were growing impatient. The group had new material for a record, and it had been three years since *Pop*.

When the long-awaited *All That You Can't Leave Behind* was released in October 2000, it debuted at number one in 22 countries and quickly sold 9 million copies. The single "Beautiful Day," which expresses a hopeful and happy message, was an instant worldwide hit. The song won three **Grammy Awards** in 2001. Three other songs from the album, "Walk On," "Elevation," and "Stuck in a Moment You Can't Get Out Of," also won Grammy Awards.

To promote the new album, U2 made more than a dozen promotional appearances. These were meant to win back mainstream fans who had deserted the band during its experimental music phase in the 1990s.

In March 2001 U2 hit the road with its Elevation tour, which sold out all 80 U.S. shows. Although U2 was back on top, the terrorist attacks of September 11, 2001, almost caused the group to cancel the third leg of its tour. This was scheduled to begin in South Bend, Indiana, one month after the attack. After deciding that music could help heal America's wounds, the band returned to the stage and played with great urgency. Audience members were moved to tears by the searing questions about pain and tragedy found in the lyrics of "Sunday Bloody Sunday." Although the song was 20 years old, it

CROSS-CURRENTS

If you want insight into a hit from *All That You Can't Leave Behind*, read "It's a Beautiful Day!" Go to page 53.

Pop and Politics

Bono meets with United Nations secretary-general Kofi Annan, left, at the United Nations Millennium Summit held September 7, 2000, in New York City. Bono, Nigerian president Olusegun Obasanjo, and officials from the Jubilee 2000 campaign presented a petition signed by more than 21 million people urging G8 leaders to cancel global debt for struggling nations.

sounded as if it had been written after the terrorist attacks. Other songs, such as "Beautiful Day" and "Pride (in the Name of Love)," also took new meanings in the wake of the tragedy. During the final song, "Walk On," the band was joined on stage by nine members of the New York City police and fire departments. Bono led them in a parade around the arena on the outer edge of the band's heart-shaped stage. Commenting on the emotional symbolism of the event, Bono asked the crowd:

> "Have you been to church? This is church."

During the 2002 Super Bowl halftime show, U2 paid tribute to victims killed during the September 11, 2001, terrorist attacks in the United States. After the band performed the song, "Where the Streets Have No Name," Bono flashed the stars-and-stripes lining of his jacket. He has worn the jacket at subsequent concerts, in tribute to those who lost their lives.

A Message of Peace

By the time U2 wrapped up the Elevation tour in December 2001, it had earned $110 million, a record only exceeded by the Rolling Stones in 1994. But the band had one more tribute to the September 11 victims. In January 2002 U2 played three songs, "Beautiful Day," "MLK," and "Where the Streets Have No Name," during the halftime show of Super Bowl XXXVI. More than a billion people watched as a 150-foot-tall curtain unfurled behind the band. During the hymnlike introduction to "Where the Streets Have No Name," the names of September 11 victims began scrolling symbolically upward to heaven. At the end of the song, Bono opened up his leather jacket to reveal the American flag lining. With that gesture, Bono united the cheering crowd.

Few other rock stars could have achieved what Bono did that day. He has deep spiritual roots and writes songs based on biblical concepts. By drawing on the healing power of music, Bono brought a message of peace to a reeling nation. And with that, the shock and the pain of September 11 seemed to vanish, if only for a moment.

Sporting his ever-present sunglasses, Bono displays his showmanship during an arena concert performance. In 2002, he took a break from concert tours to lobby politicians to offer increased funding aid to Africa, and to participate in other activities that would bring African economic, health, and educational issues to the attention of the public.

5

The Most Powerful Man in Music

AFTER A RECORD-SETTING WORLD TOUR IN 2001, Bono returned to the hard work of assisting Africa. He met with President George W. Bush, appeared on *The Oprah Winfrey Show,* and toured Africa with U.S. Treasury secretary Paul O'Neill. Bono's high-profile work earned him the title "the Most Powerful Man in Music."

Bono's efforts for Africa started after plans for a 2002 European U2 tour fell through. This allowed the 41-year-old superstar to channel his energies into his crusade. In January 2002 Bono helped found DATA, joining forces with the Bill and Melinda Gates Foundation and activists from the Jubilee 2000/Drop the Debt campaign. For the rest of the year Bono pursued DATA's agenda to provide debt and AIDS relief and promote trade in Africa. Pointing out the importance of this work in the book *U2 by U2*, Bono states:

> **"The centerpiece was AIDS, the biggest pandemic in the history of civilization. . . . Seven thousand Africans dying every day of a preventable, treatable disease is not a cause, it's an emergency."**

In March 2002 Bono traveled to Washington, D.C., where National Security advisor Condoleezza Rice introduced him to President Bush. The musician and the president discussed the African AIDS epidemic and financial assistance to poverty-stricken nations. Critics did not think the conservative president would be persuaded to consider a multibillion-dollar program proposed by an Irish rock star. However, Bush supported the cause, telling reporters:

> **"[Bono can] achieve what his heart tells him, and that is, nobody, nobody, should be living in poverty and hopelessness in the world."**

After the meeting, Bono stood next to Bush at a United Nations conference, where the president promised to increase U.S. foreign aid by $5 billion between 2004 and 2006. Bush said this sum would help eliminate poverty worldwide.

> **CROSS-CURRENTS**
>
> The U.S. plan to help Africa has been a success. To learn more about it, read "Emergency Plan for AIDS Relief." Go to page 54.

⇒ THE ODD COUPLE TOUR ⇐

Several months after meeting with the president, Bono made world headlines when he took a 10-day tour of Africa with U.S. Treasury secretary O'Neill. While Bono's previous work on the continent was purposely kept low-key, this trip was a major media event. Bono and O'Neill were accompanied by news and financial reporters, journalists from MTV and *Rolling Stone*, and Secret Service agents. They visited Ghana, Uganda, South Africa, and Ethiopia.

There was a large element of humor in the tour concerning the appearance of the two men. The conservative O'Neill was 65 and wore dark business suits. Rocker Bono had long hair and often wore

The Most Powerful Man in Music

In his efforts to promote the needs of Africa, Bono has met with U.S. president George W. Bush several times. On February 2, 2006, Bono spoke to the president and members of Congress at the National Prayer Breakfast. At the time Bono noted that the United States spends less than 1 percent of its budget on the world's poor.

his trademark wraparound designer sunglasses. Bono played up the joke, handing out T-shirts that said "The Odd Couple Tour of Africa 2002." However, Bono's mission was deadly serious. The pair toured AIDS clinics, clean-water projects, orphanages, and schools. At many stops, Bono proposed multimillion-dollar programs that would support the projects. And Bono was not shy about why he was touring with the treasury secretary, telling BBC News:

> "He is the man in charge of America's wallet. And it's true, I want to open that wallet."

O'Neill was not eager to commit millions of tax dollars to Bono's mission. But he told the press that he was passionate about increasing the standard of living for people who had been poor too long. And the very presence of a high-level American government official taking notice of Africa's problems generated goodwill. As Bono explains to the BBC:

> "We are driving down the streets and people are waving, people are jumping up and down, they are glad to see the United States."

Bono and Oprah

After returning from Africa, Bono continued to keep DATA in the news. In September he appeared with Oprah Winfrey, who some argue is as influential as the president. This made Bono so nervous he was sick in his dressing room minutes before the show. Typically, he felt better once on stage before the cameras.

Oprah asked Bono why he was so dedicated to helping Africans. He answered that when his son John was born in 2001, he became angry over the state of the world his children would inherit. Then he made his pitch to Oprah's audience, asking them to call their representatives in Washington to support DATA's goals:

> "That is why I'm on the programme. I thought if you want to speak to America, you speak to Oprah. We have to send the message that this is important. We are asking for a tiny percentage of your money."

A Gifted and Dedicated Visionary

For his selfless work with DATA, Bono was nominated for the Nobel Peace Prize in February 2003. Others nominated for the esteemed award included Pope John Paul II, French president Jacques Chirac, and equal rights activists in China, Iran, and Cuba. Bono did not win the Nobel Peace Prize, but the Recording Academy, known for its Grammy Awards, made Bono the MusiCares "Person of the Year."

The Most Powerful Man in Music

Bono appeared again on *The Oprah Winfrey Show*, when he teamed up with the television host in 2006 to promote a money-raising campaign for Africa called "(Product) Red." Various companies signed up to offer red-themed products to consumers, with the stipulation that a portion of the sales would go to the Global Fund, an organization that fights AIDS, tuberculosis, and malaria.

BONO

Bono flashes the peace sign as U2 band members celebrate receiving five trophies at the February 2006 Grammy Awards ceremony. Two of the coveted awards were for *How to Dismantle an Atomic Bomb*—for Best Rock Album and for Album of the Year. "Sometimes You Can't Make It on Your Own" won Song of the Year.

The Most Powerful Man in Music

MusiCares was founded in 1989 to help musicians in times of crisis, and its tribute dinners for "Person of the Year" raise money for the organization. The lavish ceremony for Bono in New York City was a who's who of music and political celebrities. All came to honor the Irish rocker. Guests included Bill Clinton, REM singer Michael Stipe, Fred Durst of Limp Bizkit, and Hollywood legend Robert DeNiro. In an opening speech, Recording Academy chairman Garth Fundis explained why Bono was chosen for the MusiCares award:

> **His musical accomplishments are matched only by his endeavors to effect positive change on the human condition worldwide. We truly are privileged to be honoring this gifted and dedicated visionary.**

Despite the celebrities in attendance, music was the central feature of the event. Supersonic performances of U2 songs were given by No Doubt, Norah Jones, Elvis Costello, Garbage, Mary J. Blige, and others. Bono closed the show with three songs, including an emotional version of "My Way," made famous in 1969 by Frank Sinatra.

"A Very Special Feeling"

Throughout the rest of 2003, Bono's main focus was recording another U2 album. When *How to Dismantle an Atomic Bomb* was released in 2004, fans reacted excitedly. The album debuted at number one in 34 countries and immediately sold 840,000 copies in the United States. *How to Dismantle an Atomic Bomb* was ranked as one of the best albums of the year by the *New York Times*, the *Los Angeles Times*, *USA Today*, *Q Magazine*, *Village Voice*, and others. Within a year the record sold 6 million copies.

U2 was inducted into the Rock and Roll Hall of Fame in 2005, an honor only shared by the biggest bands in music history. During his acceptance speech, Bono showed that he was not jaded from all the honors he has received:

> **It's an amazing place to be inducted in the Rock and Roll Hall of Fame, feeling like this—feeling like you've just made your first album. It's a great feeling, a very special feeling.**

BONO

❧ (PRODUCT) RED ☙

After achieving rock's highest honor, Bono continued making headlines as an advocate of social justice. In February 2006, he delivered the keynote address at the annual National Prayer Breakfast in Washington, D.C. This event, hosted by the U.S. Congress, is attended by more than 3,000 guests, including the president. In his speech, Bono described the religious beliefs that motivate him to help the poor:

At the World Economic Forum, held in Davos, Switzerland, in January 2008, Bono joined Microsoft chairman Bill Gates, left, and Dell computer founder Michael Dell, right, for a photo op. The businessmen were promoting four products—a desktop computer, two notebooks, and a printer—that were part of the (Red) initiative, which raises money for the Global Fund.

The Most Powerful Man in Music

> "God is in the slums, in the cardboard boxes where the poor play house. . . . God is in the silence of a mother who has infected her child with a virus that will end both their lives. . . . God is in the cries heard under the rubble of war. . . . God is in the debris of wasted opportunity and lives, and God is with us if we are with them. . . .
>
> "It's not a coincidence that in the Scriptures, poverty is mentioned more than 2,100 times. It's not an accident. That's a lot of air time, 2,100 mentions. [You know, the only time Christ is judgmental is on the subject of the poor.] 'As you have done it unto the least of these my brethren, you have done it unto me.' (Matthew 25:40). As I say, good news to the poor."

In 2006 Bono thought of yet another way to raise money for Africa. He launched the (Product) RED line with major corporations such as American Express, Apple, Converse, Motorola, Gap, and Armani. Each partner company created a product, such as the iPod Nano and Motorazr phone, with the RED logo. A percentage of the profit goes to the Global Fund to Fight AIDS, Tuberculosis, and Malaria, established in 2002 with the support of United Nations secretary-general Annan.

By February 2008 (Product) RED had raised more than $100 million for the Global Fund. The money helped 1.4 million Africans with treatment for HIV and AIDS, provided 2.1 million orphans with basic care, and treated 3.3 million people for tuberculosis. The money also helped pay for 46 million insecticide-treated mosquito nets, which prevent the spread of malaria. Once again Bono was able to make a financial connection between Western consumers and the needy.

VERTIGO

For his work with Jubilee 2000, DATA, and (Product) RED, Bono was once again nominated for a Nobel Prize in 2006. By this time, Bono was on the U2 Vertigo world tour. It began in late March 2005, and by the time it finished in December 2006, more than 4.6 million tickets had been purchased for 131 sold-out shows. U2 grossed more than $389 million.

BONO

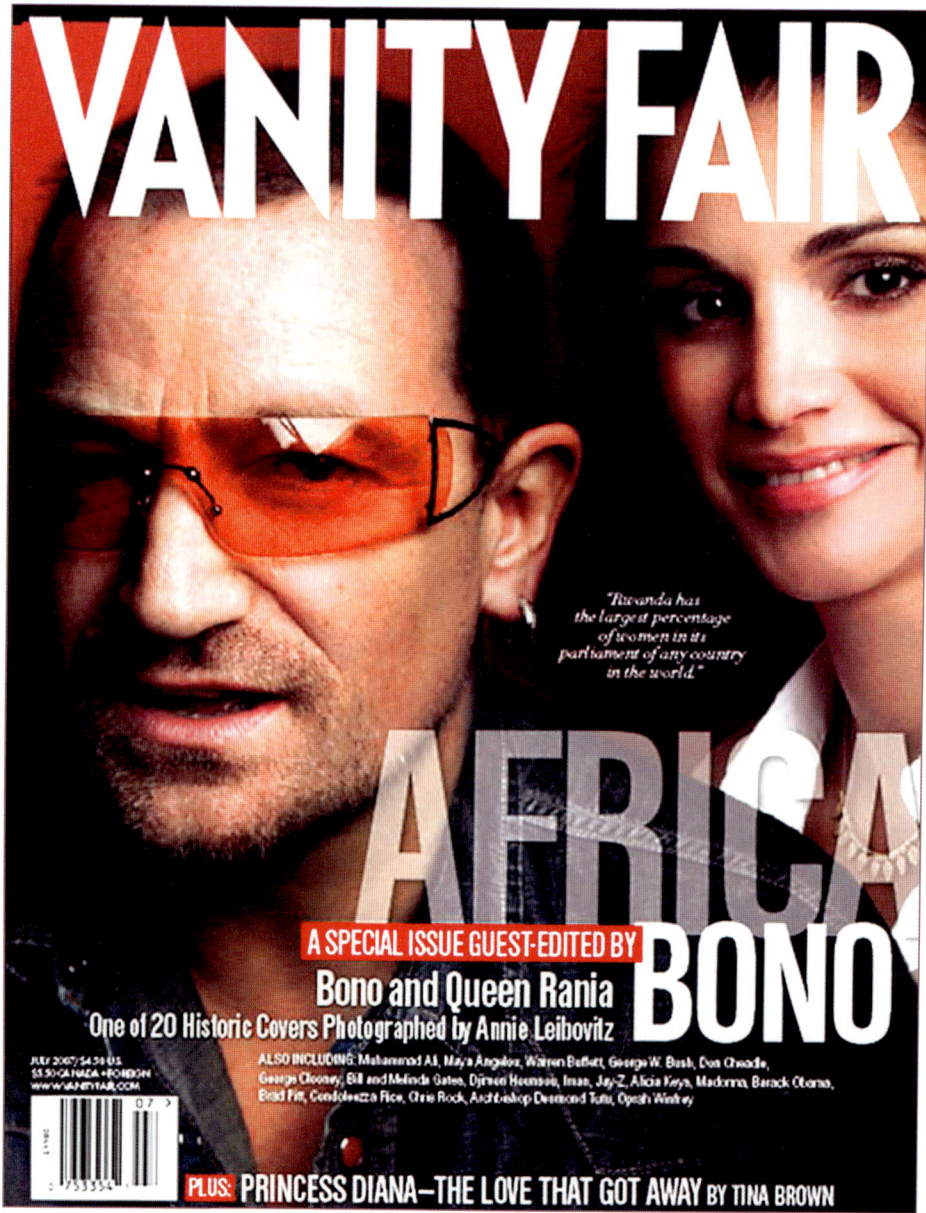

Bono served as guest editor for the magazine *Vanity Fair* for a special issue about Africa published in July 2007. Africa has much to offer, he told ABC News: "I want to do an issue about Africa where the sense is Africa: an opportunity, Africa: an adventure. Not just a burden, which is the way people normally see it."

The Most Powerful Man in Music

Several of the Latin American shows on the Vertigo tour were filmed with newly developed digital three-dimensional (3-D) cameras. The footage was used for the 2008 movie *U23D*, the first live-action film produced and shown in 3-D. This technique gives viewers an extremely lifelike concert experience in a theater.

Anyone watching *U23D* can see that Bono still loves his life as a rock star. Driven by a big ego and an even bigger heart, he has revolutionized rock and roll. But he is also saving lives and changing history, making all the world a stage for his good works. For these efforts, he stands alone among his generation. While many wealthy entertainers donate time and money to charitable causes, few can claim they have personally helped save the lives of millions of people. And Bono Vox is not through yet. As he stated in *U2 by U2*:

> **"I'm waking up every day now trying to imagine what we can do next."**

CROSS-CURRENTS

"U2 in 3-D" provides information about the history of 3-D films, and details about the band's groundbreaking 2008 concert film. Go to page 54.

AIDS in Africa

Since the 1980s, the average lifespan of Africa's citizens has fallen dramatically. As of 2008 life expectancy in sub-Saharan Africa (the region south of the Sahara Desert) had plummeted to about 47 years—considerably lower than the average lifespan of people living in East Asia (69 years) or in industrial nations like the United States (78 years). Although famine, accidents, and warfare account for some of Africa's premature deaths, much of this decrease in life expectancy is due to infectious diseases.

The greatest killer has been AIDS (acquired immune deficiency syndrome), an incurable disease caused by a virus known as HIV, which weakens the body's immune system so that it cannot fight off infections. While AIDS has spread across the globe since the first cases were identified in the early 1980s, the people of Africa—particularly sub-Saharan Africa—have clearly suffered the most. Of the more than 28 million lives lost to the worldwide AIDS pandemic through the end of 2004, approximately 26 million were Africans from countries south of the Sahara Desert. Sub-Saharan Africa contains only about 10 percent of the world's population, but it is home to more than 60 percent of all HIV/AIDS cases. And the outlook continues to be bleak: each year in Africa, the death toll from AIDS rises by more than 2 million.

In some nations of southern Africa, one-third or more of the adult population (people between the ages of 15 and 49) is living with HIV/AIDS. Botswana suffers the highest adult prevalence rate: an estimated 38.8 percent of citizens in the 15–49 age group are HIV-positive (infected with HIV). According to the United Nations, the life expectancy in nine southern African countries (Botswana, Central African Republic, Lesotho, Malawi, Mozambique, Rwanda, Swaziland, Zambia, and Zimbabwe) is less than 40 years.

In large part, Africans have been vulnerable to AIDS and other deadly diseases like malaria and tuberculosis because they are extremely poor. Most African countries are developing nations, or countries in which the majority of people live in poverty. According to the United Nations Conference on Trade and Development, almost 9 out of 10 people in the continent's poorest countries live on an income of less than $2 per day. About two-thirds live in extreme poverty, defined as an income of $1 per day or less per person. In such households, families cannot meet their basic needs for survival (food, health care, safe drinking water and sanitation, shelter, clothing), and the lack of these necessities has compromised their health.

(Go back to page 6.)

CROSS-CURRENTS

Bono and the G8

The G8 is not the name of a rock-and-roll band but stands for the Group of Eight. The organization is made up of representatives from eight of the world's richest nations: Canada, France, Germany, Italy, Japan, Russia, the United Kingdom, and the United States. These countries control about 65 percent of the world's wealth and nearly all of its nuclear weapons.

Each year the G8 holds a three-day summit for government representatives to discuss world problems. The G8 summit also attracts rock stars like Bono and movie stars like George Clooney, who attend to promote various social causes. When Bono attended the G8 in 2005, he secured promises from Western nations to double African aid from $25 billion to $50 billion. Hours after the summit, Bono commented on the success of his mission to MTV:

> **"A mountain has been climbed here. But it's worth just stopping for a second and looking back down the valley at where we've all come. Doubling aid for Africa has not been easy, and it's been a very hard sell for us salesmen. And I'm very proud to report that these figures are very meaningful."**

(Go back to page 6.)

U.S. president George W. Bush (right) confers with other G8 leaders during the first session of the 2005 summit, held July 6–8, at the Gleneagles Hotel, in Perthshire, Scotland. Upon conclusion of the meeting, the G8 leaders announced that $40 billion of debt owed by some of the world's poorest nations would be canceled. G8 leaders also pledged $25 billion in aid to sub-Saharan Africa.

CROSS-CURRENTS

Religious Tensions in Ireland

Bono's mother was Protestant and his father was Catholic. This was considered a mixed marriage in 1960s Ireland. Such marriages were unusual at the time. During this era, Ireland was the scene of much religious violence, intolerance, and hatred between Catholics and Protestants. The problems could be traced to the nation's long history of British rule.

Beginning in the 12th century, England had exerted a measure of control over neighboring Ireland. The people of both countries were predominantly Roman Catholic until the 16th century, when King Henry VIII of England broke with the Catholic Church and established his country as a Protestant nation. Henry and his successors, Queen Elizabeth I and King James I, made it illegal to be a Catholic in England. They also sent loyal Protestants to take over lands in Ireland belonging to Catholics. This tied Ireland more closely to England. Over the next few centuries, the Irish tried numerous times to break away, but were unable to defeat the superior English forces. Protestants in Ireland were given preference in government and business, while Irish Catholics often faced discrimination. In 1801, Ireland was officially made part of the Kingdom of Great Britain.

Throughout the 19th and early 20th centuries, Irish nationalists continued to work for freedom from Great Britain. In 1922 26 counties in southern Ireland, where the people were mostly Catholic, established the Republic of Ireland. The republic gained a measure of political freedom, although it still had ties to Great Britain. Six counties in northern Ireland, where more Protestants lived, elected to remain under British rule. The Republic of Ireland gained complete independence from Britain in 1949.

In 1968 Catholics in Northern Ireland staged an uprising with riots and protest marches demanding freedom from British rule. Great Britain responded by sending in military troops to reestablish order. The decades that followed were called "the Troubles." British soldiers, backed by Northern Ireland Protestant Loyalists, battled Catholic factions such as the Irish Republican Army (IRA). This low-intensity Irish civil war involved bombings, riots, bloody protests, massacres, terrorist attacks, and ethnic conflict.

Although the Troubles did not take place in Dublin, a city in the Republic of Ireland, the religious hatred intruded on the daily lives of Bono and his family. Although Bono was raised Protestant, he always felt that he was sitting on a fence, with no connection to either religion. These feelings eased when he attended Mount Temple High. It was the only school in Ireland's capital that admitted both Catholic and Protestant students.

(Go back to page 12.)

CROSS-CURRENTS

"About as Low as You Can Get"

Bono's parents grew up in the center of Dublin, Ireland, while he was raised in the city suburbs. His father was Catholic, while his mother was Protestant. Bono doesn't recall problems in his household because his parents followed two different religious traditions. But his mother's sudden death from a brain aneurysm caused a rift between his father and him that took years to heal.

After Bono's mother died, he became an extremely rebellious teenager. He argued with his father and brother, dressed like an outrageous punk rocker, and rarely obeyed household rules. Bono describes these difficult times—and some unusual acrobatics—to music journalist Michka Assayas:

"After my mother died, I think I tortured my brother and my father. There were three men living alone in a house. There were some awful times that we shared, really, about as low as you can get for three men. I remember, physically, my father trying to knock me out. I never returned fire, but it was hard. Mostly, they were comical moments. . . . I'd be seventeen, and I'd be going out to punk rock gigs, and coming back. He'd be waiting for me at the top of the stairs, with some heavy artillery *[laughs]*. It was like an obstacle course for me and my gang of friends: how to get back in the house. . . . I used to climb up the two floors on the drainpipe, and then I would reach over to the bathroom window, cross to the window—quite a tricky maneuver—put my hand in the window, open and get in, and go down, and let my friends in, so we can hang out some more."

(Go back to page 12.)

CROSS-CURRENTS

The All-Time Best Performance

In 1983 U2's concert album *Under a Blood Red Sky* became the band's best-selling record and made its members international superstars. In *Bono: In the Name of Love*, music journalist Mick Wall describes the album and the Red Rocks Amphitheatre where it was recorded:

"The venue, a natural amphitheatre set between huge, deep red sandstone boulders two miles up in the Rocky Mountains of Colorado, proved the ideal backdrop for Bono and the band to put on one of their all-time, crowd-pleasing, down-on-one-knee, flag-waving, drum-beating, belligerently best performances. The nine thousand fans there that night gave the band every encouragement, not least because several days of unseasonably inclement weather had made it odds-on the event would be cancelled. As it transpired, the torrential rain which had lashed down all day stopped just before U2 took to the stage, and the performance went ahead as planned. In 1999, influential US magazine *Entertainment Weekly* would rate this 40th in their list of 100 Greatest Moments in Rock, but for many U2 fans this spectacle has yet to be equalled." (Go back to page 21.)

Civil War in Nicaragua

In 1986 Bono traveled with his wife, Ali, to Nicaragua. The country was in the midst of a civil war, which had begun seven years earlier. In 1979 Nicaraguan revolutionaries, called Sandinistas, overthrew the country's dictator, Anastasio Somoza, whose family had ruled the country for more than 40 years. Somoza had been a cruel ruler, and the country had suffered greatly. Many of the people were poor and had little hope.

However, the United States government did not approve of the Sandinistas. This was the height of the Cold War, and the Sandinistas were allied with Communist countries like Cuba. U.S. president Ronald Reagan authorized the CIA to help create military squads to drive the Sandinistas from power. These insurgent groups became known as the Contras. The U.S. also declared an embargo, forbidding American companies to trade with Nicaragua as long as the Sandinistas were in power. The civil war finally ended with a cease-fire in 1988.

Bono visited Nicaragua in order to raise awareness of the small Central American country's problems. He wanted to help refugees and starving peasants caught in the war's crossfire. A year after Bono's visit to Nicaragua, U2 released its album *The Joshua Tree*. Many Nicaraguans believe that a song from that album, "Where the Streets Have No Name," was written about Managua, the country's capital. (Go back to page 25.)

CROSS-CURRENTS

"It's a Beautiful Day!"

In the late 1990s Bono's work with Jubilee 2000 and African debt relief took him away from U2 for extended periods. This caused tension with other band members. But when U2 got back together to record *All That You Can't Leave Behind*, Bono felt a sense of achievement. He had convinced tough-minded American politicians to join his cause. As Niall Stokes writes in *U2 into the Heart*, Bono's happiness resulted in him writing the worldwide hit "Beautiful Day":

"The Jubilee 2000 campaign that Bono got involved in was just another distraction in the course of making *All That You Can't Leave Behind*. There was frustration in the air [over] this typical Bono crusade. . . . When the Jubilee 2000 ship came in, however, Bono experienced a surge of optimism. He'd sat down with arch-conservative Congressman Jesse Helms in Washington and hit some kind of emotional nerve. Now the US had come on board, to the extent of $435 million in cancelled debts. Maybe the world wasn't such a bad place after all. There was hope. It's a beautiful day—it was a feeling rather than a thought. But when he went in to the studio, that's the way it came out, the sensation of 'connectedness,' of well being, of . . . vindication. It's a beautiful day!" (Go back to page 32.) ⏪

During the 1990s Jubilee 2000 members held protests around the world demanding the cancellation of third world debt by the year 2000. The rest of the name of the organization comes from the Book of Leviticus in the Bible, which proclaims a "year of jubilee" when those enslaved by debts will be free.

CROSS-CURRENTS

Emergency Plan for AIDS Relief

When Bono met with President Bush in 2002, he was criticized by those who did not agree with the Bush administration's conservative policies. Detractors did not believe that the president, who was consumed with his war on terror at that time, would be interested in helping poor Africans. In September 2001, just nine months after Bush had taken office, terrorists had killed some 3,000 Americans in their attacks on the World Trade Center in New York and the Pentagon near Washington, D.C.

But Bush surprised many people when, in his State of the Union address during January 2003, he proposed a major initiative to help the people of Africa. Bush proposed an "Emergency Plan for AIDS Relief" that would commit $15 billion over five years to prevent the spread of HIV in Africa and the Caribbean, and to treat Africans who had been infected with the disease.

After five years, the plan was widely considered a great success. The program helped provide AIDS treatment on a large scale for the first time, increasing the number of Africans with access to AIDS drugs from about 50,000 in 2003 to more than 1.4 million in 2008. As a result, the President's Emergency Plan for AIDS Relief was renewed in March 2008 for another five years. (Go back to page 38.) ◀◀

U2 in 3-D

Three-dimensional (3-D) movies have been around for decades. They are filmed with two cameras that are side by side, like a pair of eyes. Viewers watch a 3-D film with special glasses that help create the illusion that the action on screen is three-dimensional, rather than flat.

The first time a 3-D film was played for a paying audience occurred in September 1922. The film was called *The Power of Love*. However, the technique did not really take off until the 1950s, when several major studios released 3-D films. Interest in 3-D movies proved to be short-lived, however. For the most part, the technique was only used for low-budget movies.

In 2005, a 3-D enthusiast named Steve Schklair developed a way to shoot 3-D films using a special, high-tech digital camera. This method and equipment were used in the making of the concert documentary *U23D* during 2007. When the film was released in early 2008, many reviewers praised *U23D*'s remarkable visual sensations. The following is from the IndieLondon Web site:

> **"The film is a revolution in 3D technology. It's like having the best seat in the auditorium—but better; you're right there. So close, in fact, that you can see the zits and the sweat on The Edge's brow, or the veins in Bono's throat as he hits the high notes on *Miss Sarajevo*."**

(Go back to page 47.)

CHRONOLOGY

1960   Paul "Bono" Hewson is born in Dublin, Ireland, on May 10.

1974   Iris Hewson, Bono's mother, dies on September 10.

1976   Bono plays music for the first time with future members of U2 on September 26.

1980   U2 signs with Island Records in April, and their first single, "11 O'Clock Tick-Tock," is released a month later; U2's debut album, *Boy*, is released.

1983   U2's breakthrough third album, *War*, is released with the controversial song "Sunday Bloody Sunday."

1985   Bono gives a memorable performance on July 13, when U2 plays Live Aid at Wembley Stadium.

1987   *The Joshua Tree*, U2's fifth studio album, is released. It tops the album charts for nine weeks, stays on it for two years, and produces three hit singles.

1992   U2 begins its high-tech, multimedia Zoo TV tour on February 25.

1995   Bono works with opera singer Luciano Pavarotti to raise money for War Child.

1998   Bono plays a concert in Belfast to promote the "Yes" campaign to end the civil war in Northern Ireland.

1999   Bono begins working with the Jubilee 2000 campaign founded to erase African debt by the year 2000.

2002   In January Bono joins forces with the Bill and Melinda Gates Foundation to found DATA; Bono meets with President Bush in March and tours Africa with U.S. Treasury secretary Paul O'Neill in May.

2003   Bono is nominated for a Nobel Peace Prize.

2005   U2 is inducted into the Rock and Roll Hall of Fame.

2006   Bono launches the (Product) RED line to benefit Africa.

2008   U2 releases *U23D*, the first live-action movie shot with digital 3-D technology.

ACCOMPLISHMENTS & AWARDS

U2 Albums
1980 *Boy*
1981 *October*
1983 *War*
Under a Blood Red Sky
1984 *The Unforgettable Fire*
1987 *The Joshua Tree*
1988 *Rattle and Hum*
1991 *Achtung Baby*
1993 *Zooropa*
1997 *Pop*
2000 *All That You Can't Leave Behind*
2004 *How to Dismantle an Atomic Bomb*

U2 Videos
1984 *Under a Blood Red Sky*
1985 *The Unforgettable Fire Collection*
1989 *Rattle and Hum*
1992 *Achtung Baby*
1994 *Zoo TV Live from Sydney*
1998 *PopMart Live from Mexico City*
1999 *The Best of 1980–1990*
2001 *Elevation 2001: Live in Boston*
2003 *The Best of 1990–2000*
U2 Go Home: Live from Slane Castle
2005 *Vertigo 2005: Live in Chicago*
2006 *Zoo TV Live from Sydney*
18 Singles

Awards
1983 Brit Awards, Best Live Act

1985 MTV Awards, Best Group Video for "Pride" (nominated)

1987 MTV Awards, Viewer's Choice for "With or Without You"; Best Video, Best Group Video, Best Overall Performance, Best Director, Best Editing, and Best Cinematography for "With or Without You" (nominated)

1988 Brit Awards, Best International Group

Grammy Awards, Album of the Year for *The Joshua Tree* and Best Rock Performance by a Duo or Group for "I Still Haven't Found What I'm Looking For"

ACCOMPLISHMENTS & AWARDS

MTV Awards, Best Video from a Film for "When Love Comes to Town"; Best Video for "Where the Streets Have No Name" (nominated); Best Group for "Where the Streets Have No Name" and "I Still Haven't Found What I'm Looking For" (nominated); Best Concept for "I Still Haven't Found What I'm Looking For" (nominated); and Best Stage Performance for "Where the Streets Have No Name" (nominated)

1989 Brit Awards, Best International Group

Grammy Awards, Best Rock Performance by a Duo or Group for "Desire" and Best Video Performance, Short Form, for "Where the Streets Have No Name"

1990 Brit Awards, Best International Group

1992 Brit Awards, Best International Group

Grammy Awards, Best Rock Group Performance for *Achtung Baby*

MTV Awards, Best Special Effects, Best Group, and Best Editing for "Even Better Than the Real Thing"

1994 Grammy Awards, Best Alternative Album for *Zooropa*

MTV Europe, Best Video Award for "Stay (Faraway, So Close!)" (nominated)

1995 Grammy Awards, Best Music Video, Long Form, for "Zoo TV Live from Sydney"

MTV Europe, Best Group Award

1997 MTV Europe, Best Live Act Award

1998 Brit Awards, Best International Group

2000 Grammy Awards, Best Music Video, Long Form, for "PopMart Live from Mexico City" (nominated)

2001 Brit Awards, Best International Group and Outstanding Contribution to Music

Grammy Awards, Song of the Year, Record of the Year, and Best Rock Performance by a Duo or Group with Vocal for "Beautiful Day"

2002 Grammy Awards, Record of the Year for "Walk On"; Best Pop Performance by a Duo or Group with Vocal for "Stuck in a Moment"; Best Rock Performance by a Duo or Group with Vocal for "Elevation"; and Best Rock Album for *All That You Can't Leave Behind*

2003 Bono is nominated for a Nobel Peace Prize and is given the MusiCares Person of the Year Award.

ACCOMPLISHMENTS & AWARDS

2005   Bono is named *Time*'s Person of the Year.

           Grammy Awards, Best Rock Performance by a Duo or Group with Vocal, Best Rock Song (Songwriters Award), and Best Short Form Music Video for "Vertigo"

           Billboard Roadwork Tour Awards, Top Tour, Top Draw, and Top Single Event for the Vertigo tour

2006   Bono is nominated for a Nobel Peace Prize.

           Grammy Awards, Album of the Year for *How to Dismantle an Atomic Bomb*; Song of the Year and Best Rock Performance by a Duo or Group with Vocal for "Sometimes You Can't Make It on Your Own"; and Best Rock Song for "City of Blinding Lights"

FURTHER READING & INTERNET RESOURCES

Books
Bono et al., *U2 by U2*. New York: HarperCollins, 2006.

Anton Corbijn, *U2 & I: The Photographs 1982–2004*. Munich: Schirmer Mosel, 2005.

Pimm Jal de la Parra, *U2 Live! A Concert Documentary*. New York: Omnibus, 2003.

Niall Stokes, *U2 into the Heart*. New York: Thunder's Mouth, 2001.

Mick Wall, *Bono: In the Name of Love*. New York: Thunder's Mouth, 2005.

Web Sites

http://u2_inspire.tripod.com
The U2:Bono Web site features news and gossip about Bono, photos, quotes, interviews, and links to other Bono-related sites.

http://www.atU2.com
The U2 Web site, established in 1995, features the latest news about the band, upcoming appearances, lyrics, pictures, and band-related podcasts and blogs.

http://www.bebo.com/Profile.jsp?MemberId=2688256476
The Official U2 Fan Club, with videos, photos, a band history, and up-to-the minute news.

http://www.U2.com
The official Web site of U2, with music videos, news about tours and recordings, information about albums and lyrics, an extensive photo gallery, and links to various political groups favored by the band, including Greenpeace, DATA, Amnesty International, and Red.

http://www.u2wanderer.org
A comprehensive discography of U2, with details about the band's singles, albums, promotional discs, soundtracks, bootlegs, tribute albums, and oddities. Extensive links include a videography, U2 political causes, album images and art, and more.

Publisher's note:
The Web sites mentioned in this book were active at the time of publication. The publisher is not responsible for Web sites that have changed their addresses or discontinued operation since the date of publication. The publisher will review and update the Web site addresses each time the book is reprinted.

GLOSSARY

achtung—German for "attention."

charisma—personal charm that is used to inspire interest and affection from others.

commitment—devotion or dedication to a person or cause.

demo—a recording made by a band to demonstrate its abilities to promoters, record companies, and others.

foundation—an organization set up for charitable purposes.

front man—a person who leads a rock band and who acts as the main focus of the audience, often the lead singer or lead guitar player.

gold record—an album or single that has sold 500,000 copies as certified by the Recording Industry Association of America.

Grammy Award—an annual award given by the music industry for achievement.

moralistic—speech or writing that lectures or criticizes people about their standards of right and wrong.

platinum—an album or single that has sold over 1 million copies as certified by the Recording Industry Association of America. Albums that have sold 2 million are double platinum.

punk—a style of fast, aggressive music with stripped-down arrangements and angry lyrics that developed in the mid 1970s as characterized by the music of the Ramones and the Sex Pistols.

record producer—someone who schedules, organizes, and controls recording sessions. Producers coach and guide musicians and help mix the sound on the final product.

somber—serious, sad, marked by a dark state of mind.

synthesizer—an electronic instrument that produces an number of digital musical sounds.

techno—electronic dance music that mixes African American styles such as house, funk, electro, and electric jazz with European-style synthesizer-based music.

NOTES

Chapter 1: The Liberty Medal

page 5 "[When] you are trapped..." Bono, "Remarks on Receiving the Liberty Medal," National Constitution Center (September 27, 2007). http://www.constitutioncenter.org/libertymedal/lib_medal_bono_transcript.pdf.

page 6 "If you really want..." Josh Tyrangiel, "The Constant Charmer," *Time* (December 19, 2005). http://www.time.com/time/printout/0,8816,1142270,00.html.

page 7 "I try to live it..." Tyrangiel, "The Constant Charmer."

page 9 "Live 8 was..." "Live 8–The Long Walk to Justice" (2006). http://www.live8live.com.

Chapter 3: A Band with a Conscience

page 21 "The sight of Bono singing..." Damien Cave et al., "U2's Gamble at Red Rocks," *Rolling Stone* (June 24, 2004), p. 146.

page 22 "We broke up the band..." Mick Wall, *Bono: In the Name of Love* (New York: Thunder's Mouth Press, 2005), p. 111–12.

page 22 "U2 are involved..." Wall, *Bono*, p. 8.

Chapter 4: Pop and Politics

page 29 "To vote no..." Richard L. Berke, "Irish Feel Fierce Crosswinds as Fateful Vote Nears," *New York Times* (May 20, 1998). http://query.nytimes.com/gst/fullpage.html?res=9405E0DB1439F933A15756C0A96E958260&sec=&spon=&pagewanted=all.

page 29 "Ali and I had been..." Bono et al., *U2 by U2* (New York: HarperCollins, 2006), p. 289.

page 31 "I was part of..." "U2 Star Bono: Drop the Dept," CNN.com (January 2, 2002). http://archives.cnn.com/2002/WORLD/europe/01/01/bono.debt/index.html.

page 34 "Have you been to church..." Cathleen Falsani, "Pop Band's Lyrics Take On New Weight," U2 Tour Review (October 12, 2001). http://www.elevation-tour.com/articledetails90.html.

Chapter 5: The Most Powerful Man in Music

page 38 "The centerpiece was AIDS..." Bono et al., *U2 by U2*, p. 314.

page 38 "[Bono can] achieve..." Christina Saraceno, "Bono Meets Bush," Rollingstone.com (March 15, 2002). http://www.rollingstone.com/artists/u2/articles/story/5933712/bono_meets_bush.

page 40 "He is the man..." BBC News, "Bono Makes a Grab for US Purse Strings" (May 23, 2002). http://news.bbc.co.uk/2/hi/business/2005330.stm.

page 40 "We are driving..." BBC News, "Bono Makes a Grab for US Purse Strings."

page 40 "That is why..." Polly Graham, "24/7: Oprah Makes U2 Sick, Bono," *Sunday Mirror* (September 22, 2002). http://findarticles.com/p/articles/mi_qn4161/is_20020922/ai_n1284555.

page 43 "His musical accomplishments..." "Bono Honored as 2003 MusiCares Person of the Year," *Grammy Magazine* (February 20, 2003). http://www.grammy.com.

page 43 "It's an amazing place..." Bono, "Transcript: U2's Rock and Roll Hall of Fame Induction Speeches," U2 Station News Blog (March 17, 2005). http://www.u2station.com/news/archives/2005/03/transcript_u2s.php.

NOTES

page 45 "God is in the slums..." Bono, "Transcript: Bono Remarks at the National Prayer Breakfast," *USA Today* (February 2, 2006). http://www.usatoday.com/news/washington/2006-02-02-bono-transcript_x.htm.

page 46 "I want to do an issue..." Cynthia McFadden, Karin Weinberg, and Roxanna Sherwood, " Bono: I Want to Change the World," ABC News (June 5, 2007). http://abcnews.go.com/Nightline/story?id=3247382&page=1

page 47 "I'm waking up every day..." Bono et al., *U2 by U2*, p. 345.

Cross-Currents

page 49 "A mountain has been climbed..." Chris Harris, "Bono on G8: 'The World Spoke, and the Politicians Listened,'" MTV.com (July 11, 2005). http://www.mtv.com/news/articles/1505472/20050711/story.jhtml.

page 51 "After my mother died,..." Michka Assayas, *Bono: In Conversation with Michka Assayas* (New York: Riverhead, 2005), 18.

page 52 "The venue, a natural amphitheatre..." Mick Wall, *Bono: In the Name of Love* (New York: Thunder's Mouth, 2005), 105–106.

page 53 "The Jubilee 2000 campaign..." Niall Stokes, *U2 into the Heart* (New York: Thunder's Mouth, 2001), 147.

page 54 "The film is a revolution..." Veronica Blake, "U2 3D—Review and Bono Interview," IndieLondon (2008). http://www.indielondon.co.uk/Film-Review/u2-3d-review-and-bono-interview.

INDEX

Achtung Baby (album), **26**, 27, 28
Africa, **4**, 5–7, **24**, 29–32, 36–41, 45–46, 48, 53–54
All That You Can't Leave Behind (album), 32, 53
Annan, Kofi, 31, **33**, 45
Assayas, Michka, 51
Averill, Steve, 15

Bill and Melinda Gates Foundation, 9, 37
Bono
 awards and recognition, **4**, 5–6, 9, 27, 32, 40, **42**, 43
 birth and childhood, 10–12
 charity work, **4**, 5–9, 25, 28–33, 36–41, 43, 44–45, 47, 49, 52–54
 and Christianity, 7–8, 44–45
 education, 11–12, 51
 and formation of U2, 13–15
 marriage, 18, 25
 nominated for the Nobel Peace Prize, 40, 45
 See also U2
Bono: In the Name of Love (Wall), 52
Boy (album), 17–18, **19**
Bush, George W., 7, 37, 38, **39**, **49**, 54

Christianity, 7–8, 44–45, 50
Clayton, Adam, **13**, 14, 17

DATA (Debt, AIDS, Trade, Africa), **4**, 5–6, 9, 37–38, 40, 45

Eno, Brian, 21–22, 28–29
Evans, David "The Edge," **13**, 14–15, 17, 18, 29

Feedback. *See* U2
Fundis, Garth, 43

G8 summit, 6–7, 8, 49
Geldof, Bob, 22
The Global Fund, **41**, **44**, 45
Grammy Awards, 32, **42**

Hewson, Ali Stewart (wife), 18, 25, 29, **31**, 52
Hewson, Bobby (father), 11, 50, 51
Hewson, Iris (mother), 11, 12, 50, 51
Hewson, John (son), 40
Hewson, Norman (brother), 11, 51
Hewson, Paul David. *See* Bono
How to Dismantle an Atomic Bomb (album), **42**, 43
Hype. *See* U2

The Joshua Tree (album), 25, 52
Jubilee 2000, 30–32, **33**, 37, 45, 53

Lanois, Daniel, 21
Liberty Medal, **4**, 5–6
Live 8 concerts, 8–9
Live Aid concert, 22, 24, 25

Mullen, Larry, Jr., **13**, 14, 17
Musician magazine, **23**

Nicaragua, 25, 52

October (album), 18, **19**
O'Neill, Paul, 37, 38–40

Pavarotti, Luciano, 28–29
Pavarotti and Friends (album), 29
Pop (album), **26**, 28, 32
(Product) Red, **41**, 44–45

Rice, Condoleezza, 38
Rock and Roll Hall of Fame, 43

Sachs, Jeffrey, 30
Santorum, Rick, 6
Schklair, Steve, 54
Stewart, Ali (wife), 18, 25, 29, **31**, 52
Super Bowl (2002), 34–35

Time Person of the Year, 9
the Troubles (in Ireland), 12, 18–19, **20**, 29, 50

U2
 albums, 15, 17–22, 25–28, 32, **42**, 43, 52, 53
 awards, 27, 32, **42**
 founding of, 13–15
 and the Rock and Roll Hall of Fame, 43
 at the Super Bowl (2002), 34–35
 and *U23D* (movie), 47, 54
 See also Bono
U2 by U2, **16**, 29–30, 38, 47
U2 into the Heart (Stokes), 53
U23D (movie), 47, 54
Under a Blood Red Sky (album), 21, 52
The Unforgettable Fire (album), 21–22

Wall, Mick, 52
War (album), 18–21
War Child, 28–29
Winfrey, Oprah, 37, 40, **41**

Zooropa (album), **26**, 28

Numbers in **bold italics** refer to captions.

ABOUT THE AUTHOR

Stuart A. Kallen is a freelance author who has written more than 250 books for young adults. He lives in San Diego and is a singer/songwriter and photographer in his spare time.

PICTURE CREDITS

page

- **1:** NMI/PRMS
- **4:** NMI/PRMS
- **7:** AFP/NewsFile/Maxwells
- **8:** Live 8 Media/NMI
- **10:** Mirrorpix
- **13:** Island Records/Star Photos
- **14:** Mirrorpix
- **16:** New Millennium Images
- **19:** Mirrorpix
- **20:** Island Records/NMI
- **23:** Musician/NMI
- **24:** Mirrorpix
- **26:** Island Records/NMI
- **28:** AFP Photo/ANSA
- **31:** Reuters Photo Archive
- **33:** AFP Photo/ABRAMS
- **34:** AFP Photos
- **36:** Deutsch Presse Agentur
- **39:** Dennis Brack/Sipa Press
- **41:** (RED)/NMI
- **42:** Hahn/Khayat/Abaca Press
- **44:** (RED)/NMI
- **46:** Vanity Fair/NMI
- **49:** Eric Draper/The White House/KRT
- **51:** T&T/IOW Photos
- **53:** Melbourne J18/CIC Photos

Front cover: Zuma Press